Think! King/Queen
Why Give [It] Away?
Copyright© 2021 by April Warner

All rights reserved. No part of this book may be reproduced in any form, stored in any retrieval system, or transmitted in any form by any means, without prior permission in writing from the publisher, except as provided by United States of America copyright law.

This is a work of nonfiction. Any resemblance to actual persons, living or dead, occurrences, businesses, communities, or locales is entirely coincidental. For permission requests, email: warnerapril111@outlook.com

All Scripture quotations, unless indicated, are taken from the *Holy Bible, New King James Version* (NKJV). Copyright© 1982 by Thomas Nelson, Inc. Used by permission. All rights reserved.

Publisher: Self-published by Author

Library of Congress Cataloging-in-Publication Data has been applied for.

ISBN: 978-0-578-90616-4 (trade paperback)

Printed in the United States of America

DEDICATION

In dedication to my parents, thanks for the enriching conversations, wise, Godly counsel. I can rely on you to make things plain and simple for me to understand. When my discernment was skewed, or I didn't turn pages quick enough, you firmly taught by example while being patient with me. Thanks sincerely for showing me how to endure, live through attentively, lovingly, truthfully. I love you forever.

CONTENTS

Introduction iii

Chapter 1 - Thinking 1

Chapter 2 - Relationships 5

Chapter 3 - Unresolved Issues 10

Chapter 4 - My Testimony: A Story of Redemption 14

Chapter 5 - Resolve 21

Chapter 6 - Food for Thought 23

Chapter 7 - Plans or Strategies 24

Chapter 8 - Shift 25

Chapter 9 - Figuring It Out 28

Chapter 10 - Wrapping This Up 35

Acknowledgements 39

The Origin 40

Note to the Editor 42

About the Author 43

Think! King/Queen Why Give [It] Away?

INTRODUCTION

This book is about life experiences, encounters, and a common thread that connects us. The information contained, when utilized as responsibly as intended, develops life-changing confidence leading to making better/wiser decisions and living life powerfully. While reading, if some of the information seemingly resembles common sense, consider this, if common sense is so common, most everyone would make better/wiser decisions. Yes, people may know how to free themselves from actual dilemmas, entanglements, and precarious situations sooner; nevertheless, like playing a chess game or putting together a puzzle, we all can learn something from at least one experience or someone while growing through the journey.

    In part, I am a woman of faith, giving Almighty God all the glory that He deserves. I am not "self-made" or "self-taught." My experience of having worked in the legal profession and working in the behavioral health profession enables me to serve and to acquire knowledge, skills, and opportunities to assist with recognizing and resolving emergency/crisis issues. What puzzles me is some are unaware of the available array

Think! King/Queen Why Give [It] Away?

of services, or they refuse services. The most rewarding is hearing from those who are participating that they are benefitting from services and giving back to the community, like checkmate or completing a puzzle is satisfying.

You have probably heard, time is of the essence, time is irreplaceable, time is irretrievable, so let's continue onto the next section titled Thinking.

Think! King/Queen Why Give [It] Away?

Chapter 1

Thinking

For quite some time, one way of thinking has led to the vulnerability of being controlled by something, having a one-side-perspective, others' decisions. From my perspective, making a better/wiser decision enables individuals to prevail over one way of thinking that affects aspects of their life and others' lives. Some will, and for whatever reason, some will not decide another way. Why not? After all, there are multiple types, ways of thinking, to name a few: analytical, creative, critical thinking, which can happen at any time/moment like now.

      Why love a game or sport more than the other? Why care about something or like someone? Why contribute in more ways than one or less? Freely giving, yet nothing is received:

No high five
No fist or elbow bump
No hug
No kiss

Think! King/Queen Why Give [It] Away?

No love language

No tangible gift

Let's be honest! Recurring (repeated) lack of appreciation is just plain ol' disrespectful, perplexing. As a result, the ego can be bruised, grudgingly refuse to let go of hurt feelings. Forget about "nip it in the bud." The mind thinks about the "big payback" but skims over the idea of consequences of what happens when the same is done unto one as is done to another (sowing and reaping, karma). The heart begins to throb faster while the mind continues in thought, considering, reasoning about something. Admitting to ignoring and practicing avoidance is sometimes helpful "in the heat of the moment." Refusing to communicate or turning the other check is not as effective.

When unchecked, ineffective approaches to include avoidance can lead to anxiety, manifestations of other emotional, physical problems. There is the option of choosing to yield on the side of caution or take the "high road" instead of the "low road."

Think! King/Queen Why Give [It] Away?

What does the low road mean to you? In the moral sense, not geographical:

_____

_____

What does the high road mean to you?

_____

_____

Define giver:

_____

_____

Define receiver:

_____

_____

      More about thinking; consider, is it enough to tell children to stay away from the railroad tracks or the rickety (wobbly, unstable) train trestle? Who taught you how to discern good, bad, truths, falsehoods, real, fake? Who yelled: get out of the kitchen if it's too hot! Who helped to figure out something challenging when a friend, coach was unavailable? Sometimes the help is a parent, grandparent, sibling, or someone else. Who taught you how to fight physically, spiritually?

      As we grow, learning and discovering, life seems simple when we figure out how situations are supposed to happen and how to respond when situations happen the way we expect.

Think! King/Queen Why Give [It] Away?

Life can be like putting together a puzzle, later discovering missing pieces, or as challenging as a chess game. There are benefits of looking for missing puzzle pieces and anticipating chess moves. Both experiences assist in developing cognitive (thinking, reasoning) skills and problem-solving goals. Here is a partial list of strategic keys to achieving these goals:

- Focus - Vision, to pay attention to
- Prioritize - Treat as important, concentrate on
- Discipline – Controlled, habitual way
- Patience – Endurance, determination
- Resilience - Buoyancy, ability to recover from
- Grace – unmerited favor, help

The complexities of putting together a puzzle or playing a chess game can be as therapeutic as preparing and following through with an action plan. If you think you can, you will. The goal achieved can be more than imagined. If unachieved as anticipated, the outcome can be disappointing. I believe; masking, harboring, festering feelings are determining factors of how we respond during a lifetime. Why not prepare an action plan, at least, for the 'whatever happens just happens,' "knee-jerk" reactions before they occur? Think!

Think! King/Queen Why Give [It] Away?

Chapter 2

Relationships

Precious memories, oh how they linger. Memories of relationships, fond or not, envelopes hearts, minds. Some display enthusiasm, the pep in the step, the glide in the stride, the swag in the walk. A high-maintenance relationship looks expensive, flashy. There are power moves; some are like orchestrating chess moves. "Entanglements" do occur. Let's not forget about emotions that can be scattered like puzzle pieces all over, feelings of being on the apex (top or highest part) of a mountain and down in the valley; a single day can encompass all.

    Watching the elders make ends meet taught me: lessons about work, relationships. Sometimes they agreed with one another, produced favorable results, and sometimes not. Disciplining ones' thoughts, not flippantly saying "whatever," and going somewhere to sit down are ways of keeping a relationship peaceful. Yes dear, Yes poppy, Yes momma! Respect is given and received. I am intrigued by how someone

Think! King/Queen Why Give [It] Away?

stands firm in ones' conviction of doing things a certain way while another willingly yields. Then there is a luscious kiss on the lips, and occasionally, I see a pat on the buttocks, also known as a love tap.

Like oil and water, some relationships <u>do</u> <u>not</u> mix well. A miracle would have to bring some folk together like a Sabbath day kind-of-love; all seems well until someone hears a juicy conversation, sees a hint of drama. Just imagine puzzle pieces forced to fit together; what were we/they thinking? Unexpected situations lead to feelings of being blindsided cause love and respect to be questioned. One is open-minded to discussing issues. The other is not receptive, at least not when the other is ready to discuss. Antagonizing until getting what is wanted can be perceived as self-gratification, self-indulgence. Indeed, these types of relationships exhibit frequent misunderstandings leading to "hot" messes.

You might have guessed patterns change, for example, staying out later than usual 'chillin' with buddies, homeboys,

Think! King/Queen Why Give [It] Away?

homies, resuming nights out with BFFs, girlfriends, sisters, interests, loss of interest in certain places, people, things (including appetite). After an intense disagreement, someone emotionally detaches or leaves wanting space to think. To each their own, a deal-breaker occurs. List your deal breakers:

_____

_____

How do you handle deal breakers: fight, flight, or freeze? If the choice is to fight, is this fair?

_____

_____

If flight, now or later?

_____

If faking or doing nothing (freeze) is the response, list why?

_____

Of course, relationship issues vary: Scenario A: Someone will claim the other has bad energy. One pushes the other away. Scenario B: A couple will tangle with each other/others. Someone realizes that the other lied.

Think! King/Queen Why Give [It] Away?

Scenario C: Someone experiences "déjà vu" moments. Here we go again, repeating cycles. Then there is Scenario D: A king cat or queen feline in a prairie will get hurt. The other will attempt to heal a wound but is unable.

Moreover, being vicariously controlled in or out of a relationship occurs. Being focused on what others think about another's image, character can be emotionally draining, enervating (exhausting). Could these fixations be arrangements to distract, keep us unbalanced, designed to teach a lesson? Whatever happened to integrity building, completing honey-do lists, staying out of other people's business unless it is your household? Think!

What is the profit, purpose of trying to keep up with or forget about the Joneses when you know who fashioned, made you? By the way, the Joneses are working on being better versions of themselves.

List valid reasons for living vicariously through/coveting others and their possessions:

_____

_____

Think! King/Queen Why Give [It] Away?

The extra space below is for writing additional reasons for living vicariously through/coveting others and their possessions. If not applicable, move on. In this context, move on means turn the page.

Think! King/Queen Why Give [It] Away?

Chapter 3

Unresolved Issues

<u>Do not</u> be fooled! Unresolved issues that linger lead to misunderstandings, passive-aggressive behavior, addiction, toxic relationships. Nothing ever seems to be right; problem after problem; rarely any real solutions; consistently inconsistent; messages (verbal, nonverbal, including body language, text) are even misinterpreted, misunderstood, taken out of context. Grumbling while walking away also occurs, grumpiness.

Beware! Passive-aggressive behaviors can develop into full-grown manipulation, looking like bullying. Deep down inside, below the surface, many are attempting to quash the feelings of insecurities, repress low self-esteem. Fortunately, some are willing to admit that past/present traumas are causes for certain behaviors, responses, toxic relationships. Others will avoid/minimize issues, deny there are any issues.

Lingering unresolved issues can become daunting challenges leading to maladaptive coping,[1] which resembles emotional numbness, binge drinking. Occasionally, I ponder

---

[1] According to Merriam-Webster's Dictionary, maladaptive coping resembles avoidance behaviors such as emotional numbness, binge drinking, and social withdrawal.

Think! King/Queen Why Give [It] Away?

why some intentionally choose to "hold" on to, suppress unhealthy negative emotions for lengthy times, sometimes years, then regurgitate them on others; could this be a false sense of control, and the loss of control is evidenced by spilling over? Could zoning-out, tuning-out, marijuana use, indulging in something that numbs pain or trauma be temporary solutions to coping, quick fixes?

Unless intervention is desirous of an individual, the root cause of unresolved issues will remain hidden. Outward appearances can be deceiving as well as smiling which does not necessarily mean everything is alright. Inwardly unresolved issues lurk and can surface unexpectedly. Sharp, quick responses like "I'm fine, I'm good, I'm ok" are not necessarily conveying the truth. Maybe there needs to be a coming to Jesus meeting; have you ever heard what is hidden will be revealed or about a reveal party? Think!

Actions and attitudes are louder than words. A temper flaring, a tantrum, sore loser, poor sportsmanship conduct,

Think! King/Queen Why Give [It] Away?

"negative" behavior is worth assessing or reassessing if continuing in a relationship. Of course, a person's readiness to discuss unresolved issues will be a determining factor in its resolution. If not ready, be careful! The stink/side-eye, grimacing look, continual silence can be a sign of discontent, resentment. Anger, pain, trauma (i.e., adverse childhood experiences), flashbacks that leave a trail of unresolved issues is problematic no matter how being "in control" is perceived, portrayed.

Do you know learned behaviors can be unlearned, and regulating emotions is possible? I have learned that acknowledging root causes is an effective remedy to nurturing healthy relationships and is working for me. Relationships that are not on the brink, neither chaotic nor strained, do not need an antidote. Though wellness checks are still necessary, these types of relationships appear to be in a healthy status. Congratulations!

If not there yet (in a nurturing, healthy relationship), seek guidance when an issue is unmanageable, unhealthy, experiencing a threatening event. Tell someone trustworthy,

Think! King/Queen Why Give [It] Away?

seek physical and emotional safety. There is no time to be ambivalent (hesitant). If warranted, inform your employer, contact the National Domestic Hotline, the local police. Be receptive to life-saving options; these are defining moments.

<u>Do</u> <u>not</u> let a false sense of pride hinder or fear cause to paralyze. Sweeping stuff under a rug causes some to stumble, fall. <u>Do</u> <u>not</u> let embarrassment, guilt, intimidation, shame lead to suffering in silence. In this case, silence is <u>not</u> golden. <u>Do</u> <u>not</u> self-sabotage. <u>Do</u> <u>not</u> become your own worst enemy. Yes, hurt people turn against themselves, including others. There are exceptions to rules, and I would like to share one.

Think! King/Queen Why Give [It] Away?

Chapter 4

My Testimony: A Story of Redemption

Years ago, I was in a relationship dilemma. My partner, quite the catch, sported six-pack abs, an espresso complexion. He was eye candy. He thrilled crowds with his charisma and multidimensional approach. In my mind, I thought he could easily lift an eighteen-wheel truck with his hands, quickly talk his way out of a time-locked vault. During the first six months of dating, he was a smooth operator dripping charm until one hot summer day. When he wanted me to hang out by the pool with him and his friends, I refused and walked away. He had my car keys. He became angry, belligerent and accused me of 'cheating.' On another occasion, with nostrils flared, he accused me of "sneaking a peek" at another man. The rants increased, leading to shoves; charm faded; feeling stuck in a relationship, shame, powerlessness, was not my norm.

  The year I turned twenty, a revelation occurred; I could not change or control my partner. His quick-temper and mismanaged behavior were warning signs, red flags.

Think! King/Queen Why Give [It] Away?

Though there were signs of trouble, I did not hear any distinct warning sounds; there were no buzzers, sirens, whistles blowing. Young and naive, the thought never occurred that he would get unruly, forceful with me again; this one way of thinking skewed my perception and initial response; he did not always display his bad boy persona. The relationship continued.

Moving forward is progress, right? We decided to start a family. After receiving a positive pregnancy test, sudden suspicion confirmed an affair. The idea of continuing this relationship was questionable. We were not moving forward in the same harmonious tune. I was carrying what I will refer to as his seed, small yet significant. I began reassessing the tumultuous relationship; pondering how people reconnect after trust is broken; how can people be restored after reconnection; how can people reconcile after restoration? I also thought about the future and consequences of the pregnancy.

Reevaluating this relationship, I decided to terminate the pregnancy. My partner found proof of the abortion.

Think! King/Queen Why Give [It] Away?

He confronted me, and suddenly this encounter turned physical. His hands were wrapped around my throat, strangling me until urine trickled down my legs; my eyelids became heavier; the lights in my eyes were dimming; I could not breathe. I lost consciousness. In this case, the good news is, I woke up! Repeatedly, he was calling my name while I lay like a wet noodle on the sofa. Such as a "knight in shining armor," he lifted and carried me in his arms upstairs. Slowly laying me down on the bed, he tucked me in and faded out of the room. I quickly fell asleep. A week or so later, shortly before midnight we scuffled again. There was no time to freeze or be petrified. This fight was different from the previous fight; this time, I fought to live.

  The pivotal moment occurred when I stopped focusing on a superficial charm that was fading. I saw an opponent, started thinking strategically, and problem solved using strategic keys like listed earlier. Like moving a chess or puzzle piece in the right place, position, to get the desired result, my mind planned to protect my body from another possible encounter.

Think! King/Queen Why Give [It] Away?

Strangely, I sat down, then felt the presence of a giant standing in and near me. The fight ended just like that. He fell asleep while I stared at him for hours.

The following morning I went downstairs to call a family member. Then drove to a safe place, the Courthouse, and inquired about filing a Complaint. I received a recommendation for him and me to attend a domestic relations class; I dismissed telling him. Instead, courage and confidence accompanied me to another relative's home to discuss the incident. Within an hour after returning to my home, someone rang the doorbell. Relatives, our help, arrived and moved him out of my place. Living together for one month ended amicably. Oh, what a relief! I did not have to use the false sense of physical confidence. I safely tucked the gun away.

Physical violence was not the solution. However, when faced with no other alternative, the mind leads only to escape. I made a vow, within my heart, not to hurt anyone as I was hurt. We became friends and no more; of course, there are no promises this will happen in every case. Years later,

Think! King/Queen Why Give [It] Away?

my ex-partner apologized in the presence of two observers for his misconduct and asked for forgiveness. "You were forgiven a long time ago." Despite past adversities, the best of me overcame the vicissitudes, uncertainties, and fickleness of the relationship dilemma. There was no struggle for me to forgive.

PUZZLED?

I believe growing up in a household of faith aided in my overall attitude and behavior. Frequently attending church meetings helped. Suppose that the ability to forgive truly is innate without influences? Whether naturally or because of how each influencer nurtured me, my understanding of the power of forgiveness is that the sooner someone gives or receives forgiveness, the sooner healing begins.

I asked my Lord and Savior to forgive me for terminating (not germinating) my ex-boyfriend's seed. I believe He (my Lord and Savior) forgave me. I forgave myself. My parents do not condone abuse! Families' candid conversations help me in accepting

Think! King/Queen Why Give [It] Away?

adversaries and protectors exist. Misunderstandings, blunders, mistakes will occur, including in the workplace, sports, games, at any moment, any day.

History confirms there will be opposition, alliances, advocacies formed during a lifetime. As Movements are live and go viral, individuals are breaking their silence. People are listening, healing even through difficult times. Recovery is occurring for some, while some are still hiding, hurting.

To whom this applies, listen, seek help, contact your local authorities, file a complaint, be relentless; you do not have to live through a crisis[2] (time of intense difficulty, danger) alone. Someone will listen. Write your thoughts below, if any.

---

[2] The word crisis originates from the Greek word krisis (mashber meaning decisive moment, judgment). Krisis. (1990). In New Strong's Exhaustive Concordance, G2920: New American Standard Bible (Updated ed.). https://strong's exhaustive concordance/

Think! King/Queen Why Give [It] Away?

To all readers: list your unresolved current or past relationship issues, circle the type(s)* of relationship. If not listed, write additional types.

_____

_____

_____

*Types:

- Asexual
- Casual Sex
- Family
- Friends with benefits
- Hobosexual
- Long distance
- Monogamous
- Pansexual
- Platonic

Think! King/Queen Why Give [It] Away?

Chapter 5

Resolve

Misuse is abuse! I encourage "real" victims and abusers to tell someone, seek help. Be mindful of anyone who is perpetually bitter or sow seeds of discord; choose wisely. Communicate with someone who can help guide toward a helpful solution, someone trustworthy, someone who will be nonjudgmental, objective. Communicate to an empathetic listener. Reciprocate by listening. Thinking about a response before the speaker finishes speaking is not listening attentively. Listen.

If fabricating false narratives, why? Who are your credible others, fact-checkers, who are theirs? Are you able, qualified, willing to show or teach others (i.e., the next generation) how to live a life of accountability, integrity, responsibility? They are watching, learning, even vicariously.

My parents' candid conversations are straightforward truth, no tickling my ears, no sugar coating. "Gloves are off." Knowing they are genuinely helping (not enabling), understanding their love for me is unconditional, living through, coming out of difficult situations is part of my reconnection, restoration, and reconciliation.

"Process pain or pain will process you." Is this easy? Probably not! Some people forgive, some vow to never forget. Some <u>do</u> <u>not</u> just 'get over,' 'let things go,' move on as quickly as others. Be aware, the refusal, lack of willingness will delay healing, freedom of release, feeling a sense of peace. <u>Do</u> <u>not</u> give up. Retrospectively, I learned:

(1) People usually go through challenges before realizing their actual resiliency/strength.

(2) We have breaking points.

(3) Pain or fear can motivate, paralyze.

(4) Being patient with self is a process.

(5) Not to be afraid of candid, courageous, crucial conversations.

(6) To process resolve requires a change of mindset, behavior.

(7) Real change usually occurs inwardly, then externally.

Chapter 6

Food for Thought

Just as a thermostat is adjusted, the same is so about life. When the temperature increases, declines, or the system needs adjusting, changing will require effort. Staying in the same mental/physical state of complacency should not be an option. Mental adjustments are necessary. Moving is necessary. For example, my habit of thought and actions change when a place is extremely cold or hot for me. Instead of settling into the mindset of "it is what it is" or doing nothing, I adjust by covering with or removing a layer; if the lightweight cover-up is not enough, then a heavier weight is. Sometimes, I relocate. The nugget of this portion is: change is inevitable, as alluded to earlier.

Chapter 7

Plans or Strategies

Write your plans or strategies to resolve unresolved relationship issues that you may have listed near the end of Chapter 4.

_____

_____

_____

Write your resolutions:

_____

_____

_____

Write the names of one or more friends:

_____

_____

_____

Write names, phone numbers of additional supports. For example, counselors, family, groups:

_____

_____

_____

Think! King/Queen Why Give [It] Away?

Chapter 8

Shift

According to Merriam-Webster's Dictionary, a Paradigm Shift is a fundamental change in approach or underlying assumptions. Just imagine believing the earth is flat, then discovering that it is round; an aircraft that only flew a certain distance can now travel farther. In life, when a belief, a system such as financial, healthcare, legal, it's "always" been or done this way attitude/approach is in question, to shift from one way of thinking/doing to another is not all that easy, but possible.

Getting through requires a changed mindset, mental adjustment, reassessing matters which can lead to a physical move. Some will rely on their gut feeling/instinct, their spirit/higher power. Some focus on a mantra. What works for some might not work for others. I respond to my elders, read Scriptures,[3] pray, and meditate. Regardless of how I feel,

---

[3] "And do not be conformed to this world, but be transformed by the renewing of your mind..." (Romans 12:2, *The Holy Bible, New King James Version*, copyright© 1982 by Thomas Nelson, Inc.).
Ibid, "let no corrupt word proceed out of your mouth, but what is good for necessary edification, that it may impart grace to the hearers" (Ephesians 4:29, NKJV).

Think! King/Queen Why Give [It] Away?

self-examination compels me to seek and follow instructions of the Word of God, the Holy Spirit. I admit, my feelings <u>do</u> <u>not</u> always want to obey.

Letting go of a fixed mindset is almost as challenging for some as is letting go of bragging rights for others. According to some, the thought of thinking another way is stressful, problematic. Many have done things the same way for so long and are simply not willing to adjust. Some view a shift such as those listed already, including relationship shifts, as an opportunity to grow and learn.

Decide your method of handling a crisis, a shift, an unexpected/unplanned occurrence. If thinking the idea of being "too old," "set in your ways," not having enough resources makes you reluctant to do anything, why think that way? Remember, there is more than one way of thinking.

Doing nothing should not be an option. Examine your methods of handling a crisis, unexpected/unplanned occurrence. Are they healthy choices? Yes or No. Are they attainable? Circle Yes or No.

Think! King/Queen Why Give [It] Away?

List several accomplishments:

_____

_____

_____

List a challenge or a couple of insights about yourself. If you can't think of any, ask someone who is not afraid to be respectfully honest:

_____

_____

_____

Think! King/Queen Why Give [It] Away?

Chapter 9

Figuring [It] Out

A common thread that connects us, relationships, playing a chess game, putting together puzzle pieces, is time. Understanding time is of the essence, irreplaceable, time is irretrievable, a precious commodity, why are we misusing time/moments when there is an appointed time, opportune moment (Kairos) to work toward reconnecting, restoring, and reconciling relationships? The appointed time can be now. Why misuse time/moments by playing calculated mind games to entrap, trick, deceive each other?

Think! Kings/Queens, sons, daughters, children of the Most-High God, why give [it] away in vain. It can be your body, essentials, identity, inheritance, land, position of authority, whatever you value. "Why give [it] away" in exchange for being in unhealthy, toxic relationships, blocked, ghosted, devalued after used? Why give [it] away in exchange for money? Why relinquish, surrender God's property to coercive, Jezebel seducing, egotistical spirits, false prophets, vagabonds, wolves embodied in sheep's clothing? Why idolize people,

Think! King/Queen Why Give [It] Away?

places, things, give your cookies, valuables, jewels to swine? Think this cannot happen? The very acts that some said they would "never" do, they "did." "Keep on living." One of the richest, wisest who ever lived, King Solomon, was not even exempt[4] from erring, sin, vulnerability.

<u>Do</u> <u>not</u> give up! There is hope; like finding missing pieces of a puzzle or moving the last chess piece in the right place, position, there are practical solutions to help us build a divine relationship and protect God's property. Someone said, "the shortest distance between two points is a straight line," so let's go directly to the first of two points.

Point One - In the midst of all, trust God with your heart. The heart is the ruling center where actions, behaviors, and thoughts begin, the place where our mind, consciousness, emotions, and our will reside. When life happens, racing thoughts occur, losing self-control, "knee-jerk" reactions, manipulating, and sometimes not even trusting oneself to do

---

[4]"Thus Solomon's wisdom excelled the wisdom of all the men of the East and all the wisdom of Egypt. For he was wiser than all men...His heart turned away from the Lord" (1 Kings 4, 1 Kings 11, NKJV).

Think! King/Queen Why Give [It] Away?

what we know is right occurs, we can completely trust the God of mercy, God of love. Why? Because He is not just like any other person, man. He is not just like the smooth operator described earlier. He is not just like the person with the swag in the walk. He is a believer's rescuer. Jesus is our help.[5]

Point two - In the midst of all, trust God with your whole heart and mind. The mind is the faculty of consciousness, thought, and reasoning. I remember a saying, 'the mind can play tricks on you.' My response to that is, whether within the mind or the heart, examine, study and test all things. For example, in the Chapter Titled Thinking, who said the train trestle was "rickety?" A trustworthy source, someone's act of love told us. Also in the same chapter is the word discern. What does this mean? Discern is to perceive, distinguish; a seer sees supernaturally, help given by the Holy Spirit. Do not believe lies. To discern is not concocting/brewing something, casting spells as is practicing sorcery, witchcraft.

---

[5] "that if you confess with your mouth the Lord Jesus and believe in your heart that God has raised Him from the dead, you will be saved. For with the heart one believes unto righteousness and with the mouth confession is made unto salvation" (Romans 10:9-10, NKJV).

Think! King/Queen Why Give [It] Away?

All in all, we can completely trust the Lord. Have you tried Him? As for me, I know Him to be the greatest of all time; heart-fixer, mind regulator.

In your mind's eye, imagine a sea full of waterproof puzzles and chess pieces floating. Pieces of disappointments, images of trolls, fantasies about memory lane that perhaps lead to feeling powerless, frustrated, prostituting, masturbating. Enough is enough! If stinkin' thinking, remember there is more than one way of thinking. Focus on cleanliness/holiness. Circumstances, situations, and a willing soul can change.

Now imagine the plethora of waterproof puzzles and chess pieces imagined earlier dissolve. Distractions reduced are no longer overwhelming. Concentrate, the water recedes. The coast is clear. A repentant heart, a renewed mind forgives at least for thinking change was/is not possible. In the event some issues reoccur, do you know that does not invalidate Gods' grace and mercies on all?

There's still time to repent of sin; turn toward the God of our salvation, away from idols. If we are new creations,

Think! King/Queen Why Give [It] Away?

we are born again believers. If not born again yet, being transformed by the renewing of your mind can lead to water, Spirit, and fire baptisms preparing all of God's children for entry into new life; no baptism; no entry into the Kingdom of God, Kingdom of Light.

A "reprobate mind" will refuse to repent, detest, reject the Lord, cannot, does not glorify the King of kings, Lord of lords; well-rehearsed, and seemingly rational will try luring, leading anyone out of light toward some other source/force, astray. Indeed, there will be conflicts, "spiritual warfare." The flesh will rage against the Spirit, the Spirit against the flesh. The kingdom of darkness against the Kingdom of Light, dragon vs. Heavenly Hosts/ man/woman. Be encouraged; this is not how this story ends.

Reaching out to and receiving those who have our best interest at heart (spiritual leaders, family, friends) to help assist us through life's journey, to live as victors, not as victims, is another part of reconnection, restoration, and reconciliation. Remember, silence is <u>not</u> always golden. Communicate the need for help. We all need help sometimes.

Think! King/Queen Why Give [It] Away?

When in my past relationship dilemma (referred to in My Testimony), I needed extra help. I did not realize then but do now the giant that I felt in and near me helped me to level up extraordinarily; in spirit, I surrendered my all (body, soul, and spirit) to Almighty God. Like many generations before us who tarried all night, I remained in the posture of watching, praying until everything about that situation changed. The empowered rook (I) defeated the opponent without compromising or giving anything away to the opposition.

My prayer is that we forgive ourselves for giving [treasured possessions] away in vain, that we forgive others, make better/wiser decisions, understand we are "complete,"[6] continue praying and fasting for a spiritual breakthrough to break soul ties not authorized by the omnipotent God to connect to us. Heavenly Father, I thank You for empowering us to do great things in the name of Jesus Christ. Amen.

---

[6] "for in Him dwells all the fullness of the Godhead bodily; and you are complete in Him, who is the head of all principality and power" (Colossians 2:9-10, NKJV).

Think! King/Queen Why Give [It] Away?

Kings/Queens, lift your crown! Not because someone says, but because you are able. Declare the pity party is over! Must you cry; tears are signs of a breakthrough, release. If a war cry, shout out to the Lord! Shout! A little whine might not be enough to make anyone feel better. An excessive amount of liquid courage might get us into trouble, but it's not unlawful to declare victory is ours! Go ahead, dance even if it's undignified; just don't dance or side-step around answering these last set of questions before wrapping this up: Are you in a sensual (carnal) or spiritual relationship?

Circle Yes or No.

Circle the one that you feed the most.

Do you have fake identity accounts?

Circle Yes or No.

If yes, how often do you give in to the influence of the account(s)?

Think! King/Queen Why Give [It] Away?

Chapter 10

Wrapping This Up

Life is full of influences impacting us in many ways: sight, sound, scent, size, colors, like gold, red, and purple (which biblically symbolize kingship, royalty, holiness). Influences are impressionable. Directly or indirectly, influences and influencers will affect us. There are positive and negative effects; there is positive and negative energy all around us. Opposites, positives, and negatives will attract, repel. We will make mistakes. We will be vulnerable. We will give [valuables] away. Nonetheless, there is hope.

Giving [treasured possessions] to the King of kings, Lord of lords, will not lead to lack. Like finally putting together all pieces of a puzzle or moving that last chess piece in the right place, position, giving ourselves entirely to the life-giver and sustainer of 'all' life as He intended is the significant part of reconnection, restoration, and reconciliation of a divine relationship. It would be remiss not to admit there will be moments: fondly cherished, unforgettable memories, agreements, disagreements with Him and others, no need to worry.

Think! King/Queen Why Give [It] Away?

Responsible stewards harnessing God-given power and authority without compromising or succumbing to influences, influencers, or pressures of life live powerfully. We are 'powerful' in the city, 'powerful' in the field. Did you know, when in the wilderness, when nailed to a tree on the Hill of Golgotha/Calvary (place of execution), Jesus harnessed his power and authority? If His Father's will, He could have invoked/summoned thousands of angels, came down off the tree/cross to deviate from God's plan for us to receive the infilling of the Holy Spirit.[7]

I am so glad that is not the end of His story. Jesus obeyed His Father's will onward through His crucifixion. He conquered death and the grave, descended into the depths of the earth, ascended into heaven, is seated at the right hand of His Heavenly Father (Psalm 110:1, Hebrews 10:12, NKJV), and together we share in His resurrection. In exchange for His life, for the shedding of His blood taking us from sin to righteousness, His accusers

---

[7] "Or do you think I cannot now pray to My Father, and He will provide Me with more than twelve legions of angels?" (Matthew 26:53, NKJV).

Think! King/Queen Why Give [It] Away?

(unbelievers) saw what they wanted; His people, we (believers) received what was/is needed, empowerment of the Dunamis, Exousia, Holy Ghost power. Check your connections.

Assuredly being in fellowship/relationship with Jesus Christ, the King of kings, Lord of lords, sharing Christ's life (in sweet communion with the Holy Spirit), we are in our rightful position. We are optimistic, not fearful of doing what He intended for us to do. We are determined, not defeated by the opposition, our feelings, pride, or getting in our own way. We are the authentic power couples journeying through life not solely by sight but by faith. Amid a crisis, our faith in the power of God should not diminish but increase. As stated in the *Holy Bible*, Hebrews 11:6, "But without faith, it is impossible to please… [God]. Do not be afraid![8] Do not shrink back.

---

[8]"For God has not given us a spirit of fear, but of power and of love and of a sound mind" (2 Timothy 1:7, NKJV).
Ibid, "Behold, I give you the authority to trample on serpents and scorpions, and over all the power of the enemy, and nothing shall by any means hurt you" (Luke 10:19, NKJV).

Think! King/Queen Why Give [It] Away?

Kings/Queens, a good steward disciplining oneself, cloaked in the strength and power of the Lord, presses with determination inward/draws nearer to the Word of God, listen with the ear of your heart, surrender to Him, or are you desirously wanting to be entrenched with a crafty, influential entity treating you like a 'mere' pawn or puzzle pieces, controlling your moves/life, hindering you from making better/wiser decisions?

Think!

Think! King/Queen Why Give [It] Away?

ACKNOWLEDGEMENTS

Thanks to the elders for opportunities to glean "pearls of wisdom." Thanks to all that expect nothing but the best for and from me, for encouraging me to write, for teaching me in-depth lessons about honesty, trickery, and spirits (non-alcohol and alcohol). These life lessons are priceless. A special thanks to God-fearing consultants for helping to sharpen iron. Based on what the Author and Finisher of my faith said, "because of Him, the best of me that has always been in me is coming out of me." He has commissioned me to continue spreading the gospel, not garbage or gossip. Stories can be liberating. Have you considered sharing yours?

Think! King/Queen Why Give [It] Away?

THE ORIGIN

The origin of this book was a letter titled "It Hurts." A 12-year long-distance relationship ended. Comparable to the perseverance of the Woman with the issue of blood, I was hopeful. My heart and mind knew I would live. Read more about the Woman's story in the *Holy Bible* Matthew, Chapter 5, NKJV.

While talking to a friend, I cried. Talking about my feelings and disappointment, my friend listened while I processed pain. The pain subsided, and as time passed, my healing continued. No longer in psychological bondage by the long-distance soul tie, I chose to be free. Continuing to type "It Hurts," I later gave a handful of my closest friends and relatives a copy of the letter.

Listening to and obeying my Heavenly Father, waiting, revising, editing, updating, rewriting, and giving my editor numerous drafts, something was happening. The seeds of writing a book planted decades ago began breaking through and sprouting. Feelings of inspiration and purpose were deeply rooted. I had the fortitude and momentum to continue writing.

Think! King/Queen Why Give [It] Away?

Finally, like a flourishing tree, the letter grew into a book. The book, in part, is a testimony of one's life experience, encounters, a common thread, God's amazing grace. My testimony is to help someone, not a testament to cause division, not to offend anyone. I am still evolving and understand that God is not finished with me yet.

Think! King/Queen Why Give [It] Away?

NOTE TO THE EDITOR

Vic,

Thanks for helping to guide me profoundly during this journey. I appreciate your loyalty, perseverance, and willingness to toil together beyond the time of slap-happy sleepy and when you were physically aching. Thanks for encouraging me to continue onward soldier, working towards sharing this product, especially when I said, this is it, finished. I believe your conviction to see fruit produced, the good news shared, made this journey more worthwhile, and for that reason, I now have a broader understanding of what ensuring the mission is accomplished means to veterans like you. You are vicious.

Salute!

Think! King/Queen Why Give [It] Away?

ABOUT THE AUTHOR

April Warner was born and raised in an 'everybody knew everybody' neighborhood. Most of the influential people in her life lived nearby. Many generations were instrumental in helping April's parents to raise her and her siblings. In Ohio, under the leadership of the late Pastor Richards, April organized, facilitated, and mentored the first youth group at the church. Years later, April relocated to Virginia. During her journey, she became the manager of her own company. She and her business associate established and strengthened relationships until they decided to close the business. For more than a decade, April served as a hospice volunteer for more than thirty patients and their families. Her leadership position in the community and decades of employment in Human Services gives April opportunities to serve the citizens of Virginia, their family/friends, vendors, and the public. Visiting rehabilitation centers gives her opportunities to connect, encourage, and interact with individuals who are sick or shut-in. She enjoys playing Bingo, Pokeno (the game with the funny name) with residents and their

Think! King/Queen Why Give [It] Away?

families, receiving Cha-Cha-Cha dance lessons during her visits, putting together puzzles, serving by giving manicures/pedicures, listening to stories about wars, and stories about tying tobacco. April cherishes every moment. She enjoys, dancing, reading, singing, smelling the 'flowers,' and traveling. As a mother, April is grateful to be a parent. Her sons are indeed abundant blessings from God. She loves the Lord with her whole heart, mind, and soul. No matter what her natural eyes see, she puts all of her trust in Him.

Contact the author at:
warnerapril111@outlook.com
acooper0047@email.vccs.edu

www.ingramcontent.com/pod-product-compliance
Lightning Source LLC
Chambersburg PA
CBHW042349300426
44109CB00034B/31